HOW TO GET FILTHY RICH

Business Strategies
and
Money-making Tips
for
Success in the Real World

By HUGH BORG

Printed in the United States of America

ISBN 978-0-9897372-7-2 (eBook)
ISBN 978-0-9897372-8-9 (pbk)

Alexia Publishing
PO Box 120942
Nashville, TN 37212

www.AlexiaPublishing.com

info@alexiapublishing.com

Dollar signs
Are the greatest signs of all.

Table of Strategies

HOW TO GET FILTHY RICH

Business Strategies
and
Money-making Tips
for
Success in the Real World

Strategy 1:
Embrace Capitalism

A free market economy can be defined as an economic system in which prices and wages are determined by unrestricted competition between businesses and by supply & demand, with little or no government interference.

Capitalism is an economic system characterized by private or corporate ownership of capital goods, by investments that are determined by private decision, and by prices, production, and distribution of goods that are determined mainly by competition in a free market.

The United States economy operates as a capitalistic system. It is also considered by many to be a free market, although it is not, in the strictest sense, as there are some government controls in place. But the key point to take away from all of this is that, generally speaking, making money in western society (and some other parts of the world) is *competition-based.*

Now consider this simple question: In any competition, who usually wins? The winner is almost always the person who is stronger, faster, smarter, or simply more aggressive. Therefore, if you want to succeed and beat your competition, you must be *that person*, the one who is stronger, faster, smarter or more powerful.

It's time for a return to the principles and strategies presented in this book, the very ones that made America into an arrogant (rightly so) superpower like no other; and created scores of brash, millionaire moguls and eccentric, billionaire tycoons. Embrace this true spirit of capitalism and the free market society. Embrace it with all your heart, mind and strength; and in so doing, you will destroy your competitors and become filthy rich!

Strategy 2:
Live Like an Animal

The expression 'survival of the fittest' was coined by British sociologist Herbert Spencer in 1852, and later embraced by Charles Darwin, Adolf Hitler and Kaiser Wilhelm. Regardless of one's stance on the concept, there is no denying its validity. All living creatures on Planet Earth abide by one constant principle: Only the strong survive and prosper.

Therefore, if you want to succeed in business and get filthy rich, you must apply this truth to your life and business practices. There is no room for weakness on the path to success. You will either be the lion or the zebra, the wolf or the rabbit. You must take an aggressive, predatory stance toward your competition, or you will be the one who gets devoured. The lions and wolves are the conquerors, the ones who claim the spoils of victory and feed on the carcasses of their victims.

If you doubt this truth at all, ask yourself these questions: When was the last time you saw a rich and powerful zebra sitting on the throne as King of the Serengeti? When was the last time you saw a rabbit running around the neighborhood proclaiming himself to be CEO of a multi-billion-dollar corporation? And, have you ever seen a mouse swallow a snake or a butterfly devour an eagle? Of course not. In nature, the meek and weak animals finish last. They get eaten.

The same applies to humans. In a world that is dog-eat-dog, you must learn to be the hungrier and more ferocious dog. In a business environment based on survival of the fittest, you must be stronger and better than your opponent in order to be the last man standing. Don't get walked on; be the walker, not the walkee. Learn this vital lesson from the animal kingdom and apply it to your daily life and business practices.

Strategy 3:
Manipulation Optimization

Manipulation may have a bad connotation to some people, but it is actually a wonderful thing. Manipulation is the practice of using other people to accomplish your goals. What could be better than that?

To do this effectively, you must study other people to learn what makes them tick. Discover their weaknesses and use them against them. There is nothing more satisfying than playing on someone's emotions in order to sell them your product.

One of the simplest and most basic examples of this strategy is when a woman implies that there may be some sort of sexual reward for her man if he watches *The Notebook* or *The Bridges of Madison County* with her. The man will, of course, hastily bend to her wishes in hopes of receiving said reward. This is a classic case of simplistic manipulation.

For an example of more complex manipulation on a large scale, you might consider how Adolph Hitler played on his own people's fears, prejudices, and spirit of nationalism in order to brainwash and manipulate an entire nation to accomplish his own evil purposes of world domination. In more recent times, a similar type of manipulation has been perpetrated on an even more massive world-wide scale by teen pop idol, Justin Bieber.

Some old-time preachers were also experts at this strategy. They routinely worked their crowds into a fever-pitch of overwrought emotion until they had people weeping for lost loved ones or trembling in fear at the prospect of being cast into the fiery, burning pits of Hell!

Many a convert has been won by this fearsomely effective tactic. And don't think for a minute this strategy is unique to the Christian faith or the evangelical movement. Fear, exaggerated emotions, and oppression are used by all the religions of the world to keep the flock in line and to win new converts.

You can also learn this tactic from the very best, by watching the greatest professional manipulators of all – politicians – as they successfully put this into practice on a daily basis by pandering to and playing on the fears and misconceptions of their constituents. In so doing, political leaders are able to gain followers and convince them to swallow their particular ideology – hook, line and sinker!

Many of the greatest persuaders in history were experts at plucking the heartstrings of their target audiences. Preachers, politicians, car salesmen, insurance agents, and salespeople of all types know how to close a deal with a heart-wrenching story about a sick child, our troops fighting in a foreign land, or a young mother of three who is valiantly battling cancer. If you want to become filthy rich, you must follow their example, and do whatever it takes to manipulate customers into buying what you're selling.

Strategy 4:
Embrace Your Inner Butthole

Look around at the richest and most successful people in the world. What do they have in common? The answer is that most of them are pushy, arrogant, selfish buttholes. They're the kind of people who aren't afraid to be a horse's ass or a total jerk, if necessary, in order to achieve their goals and get what they want. They truly don't care what people think of them.

For many of us, this is the sticking point. We worry too much about how others will view us. *What will our relatives think of us? What will the neighbors say? How will my co-workers treat me if I transform from Mr. Nice Guy into a Jerk who ticks off people?* These are the fears we often tend to focus on. And while we're expending our precious energies on this fruitless endeavor, the aggressive jerk is out there closing deals, pushing through doors, accomplishing his goals, and getting filthy rich.

Don't let that happen to you. Embrace your inner butthole. Don't be afraid to become a great big annoying jerk!

Strategy 5:
No Explanation Necessary

Many people feel as though it's important for them to explain their behavior, as if all their actions have to be justified. But you mustn't worry about the opinions of others or allow yourself to fall prey to this distractive practice. In the final analysis, it's no one's business what you do or why you do it, as long as you're not physically harming anyone else. And the time you spend explaining yourself is wasted time when you could be making another large pile of money.

Remember that, typically, when people complain about your behavior, it's simply because they're jealous. They observe you taking control of your life, your financial future, and your destiny; and this, of course, makes them feel worse about themselves and ashamed of their own lack of initiative. But rather than improving their own behavior, they will often choose to whine about or deride yours. That's because most weak-willed individuals are always looking for "an easy out." I urge you to simply disregard these cretins. You owe them absolutely no explanation for your empowered attitude and life.

And if you wish, you can remind them that if they don't like what you're doing, they may avail themselves of the opportunity to place a wet smooch upon your hind quarters.

Strategy 6:
Possessions Make You Look Cool

People respect a person who has lots of stuff – such as sports cars, mansions, jewelry, paintings, and sculptures – because these items represent power and wealth. This is a basic principle that cannot be denied by even the most dim-witted individual.

Everybody wants to be *that guy*, the one who can acquire huge piles of sparkly, shiny, and outrageously expensive possessions. And if they can't *be* that guy, then they want to be friends with him, do business with him, or at the very least, be invited to his embarrassingly lavish dinners and cocktail parties. Believe me; by following this strategy, you'll suddenly have more "best friends" than you can shake a stick at! And most importantly for you, the more friends and acquaintances you acquire, the more people you'll have available to you to take advantage of!

Even if you care little for the possessions themselves, it's important that you accumulate as many of them as you can and display them as often as possible. Here are several practical examples:

(1) Wrap yourself in real furs and excessive bling at all times, even during church, Thanksgiving dinner, or a game of pickup basketball.

(2) Carry huge wads of cash in your pocket and pull it out for all to see when you pay for even the smallest of items such as a mocha latte or a pack of gum.

(3) Surround yourself with an impressive entourage no matter where you go, even if it's only to the bathroom.

Remember: the more possessions you pile up, the more impressive you appear. And the more impressive you appear, the more you will dominate in life and business. And the more dominant you are, the more heaping piles of money you will acquire, until eventually, you become absolutely stinking, filthy rich!

Strategy 7:
SEX

Sex is a topic that many prudish people would rather not discuss, and the power of sex in the business world is something that most folks often prefer to sweep under the rug. In their dream-world, la-la land, everyone is naïve, puritanical, kind, honest and generous to a fault; and no one uses sex to gain favor, close a deal, advance their career, or make money. Hate to break it to you, Alice, but this is nothing but a huge poppycock!

In the real world, most things can be and often are accomplished more quickly and effectively via carnal flirtations and outright sexual favors, rather than hard work, decency, honesty, or "above-board" practices. Many stars (and others) in the film and television industries succeeded because of sexual favors they were willing to perform. Many singers, musicians and others in the music business prospered because of their sexual prowess or deviancies. Those in the governmental arena commonly employ sex as part of the political process. And a wide variety of other craftsmen and workers – such as plumbers, livestock transporters, electricians, faucet distributors, carpet cleaners, and pizza delivery guys – often get work as a result of their sexual aggressiveness and exploits.

Face the facts about sex: Your competitors use it, people in all walks of life use it, and almost every great and successful person in history used it. So if you truly want to make tons of money, you will immediately incorporate the incomparable power of sex into your business life. Your method could be as simple as playful flirtations and innuendos between you and a customer; or it could involve a variety of small sexual favors, fetish indulgences, or video-cam demonstrations. Or, on a large scale, you might opt to utilize the full-blown services of prostitutes, transgenders, or dominatrices for your clients.

Of course, I must remind you that you never want to do anything illegal. (I am *not* winking. Or am I?) But in the highly competitive, cut-throat world of business, you must be willing to do whatever it takes to gain favor, influence people, make sales, and build your financial empire!

Sex sells. Sex is powerful. Sex is a weapon like no other, and everyone is susceptible to its allure and sting. There is no one in the entire world who wouldn't like to have more sex in any and every form possible. This is a gold mine of opportunity just waiting for a clever business-person like you to exploit. I can state unequivocally that anyone who fails to utilize the incredible power of sex is doing themselves and their business a disservice. Nothing can enable you to accomplish your goals, climb a corporate ladder, close deals, and get filthy rich as quickly and effectively as sex can.

Strategy 8:
A Lie Is Just a Different Version of the Truth

Lying is part of the fabric of our society, and most definitely an integral part of normal business operations. It's built into everything that companies do. For example, consider how many thousands or millions of times in your life you have heard the expression "New and Improved" used to describe a product. Do you really think those companies actually changed anything of substance in that product? Of course they didn't. It's all a marketing gimmick, a big fat lie.

Or, consider the price put on any given product by a store. The company wants you to believe that the amount listed is a fair price, and that they have done their very best to give you, the consumer, a great deal. It's called sales-speak, and it's a complete and utter falsehood. All companies charge as much as they can, gouge their customers as often as possible, and laugh all the way to the bank.

People pay lip service to the antiquated idea that lying is bad, but in truth, it's a necessary part of the path to success. Everyone embellishes a story, stretches the truth, exaggerates their accomplishments, dodges tough questions with misdirection, and tells little white lies whenever necessary to avoid conflict or to get what they want. Think of it this way: one person's lie is simply another's person's unique perspective on the truth.

Don't balk at this concept; accept the fact that lying is often one of your best weapons in the battle to succeed.

Sometimes you simply have to tell your customer exactly what they want to hear, even if it's not the truth. Other times it will be necessary to deceive your competitors in order to gain the upper hand. If you want to get filthy rich, you're probably going to have to lie.

Strategy 9:
Steal When Necessary

Many great authors, songwriters, musicians, and other types of artists have often stated that they stole ideas, arrangements, or musical riffs from others. Many of the great thinkers, philosophers, and inventors of all time borrowed or built upon (stole) the concepts or designs of their competitors or predecessors – Charles Darwin from Spencer, Thomas Edison from Tesla, Henry Ford from Olds – and then claimed the credit for themselves. It's a practice as old as mankind itself. Face it; the guys who invented the wheel and discovered fire probably stole the idea from another, less aggressive caveman!

The lesson here is to always keep your eyes and ears open to great, money-making ideas being conceived or developed by other people. When possible, take their general concept and enhance it, modify it, and make it your own. There is no time or need to re-invent the wheel when someone has already done it for you. And don't feel bad about taking an idea or design from your competitor. Remember this: if he could, your competitor would steal from you; you're just beating him to the punch. Besides, if your competitor isn't smart enough to protect himself from a thief, then he deserves to have his idea stolen.

Strategy 10:
Take Advantage of Every Person And Situation

Successful people understand the importance of taking advantage of every person they meet and every single situation in which they find themselves. Don't let opportunities pass you by. Never be one of those people who hang back in the crowd, like a bystander at the scene of an accident. Instead, be like the opportunistic attorney who wades in among the victims and hands out his business card. Don't just watch things happen – get involved and take advantage of the situation.

In every circumstance, there is something or someone that can be exploited or taken advantage of. And somebody is going to make use of that opportunity; why shouldn't it be you? Bear in mind, on a deeper, psychological level, some people actually *want* to be taken advantage of. By doing so, you are fulfilling something their psyche craves. You're actually doing them a favor!

Some people may decry this sort of behavior and call it tacky or uncouth, but it's actually resourceful and makes smart business sense. Always remember the old saying: *You snooze, you lose.* Some stand by and *watch* the action, while some *take* action! And it is the latter, those opportunistic individuals, who will be the ones to get filthy rich.

Strategy 11:
No is a Four-letter Word

The people who get filthy rich never give up. *Never* give up. When they hear a *No* response from a client, potential customer, supplier or anyone else, it doesn't register in their brain the same way it does to regular people. In fact, the word *No* is like a filthy, dirty, four-letter word to them. They simply ignore it and move on to their next sales pitch or persuasive argument or whatever the case may be.

Other people would normally take the hint and stop at these obvious roadblocks. But these driven individuals hop in their bulldozer and plow right through them and anyone who gets in their way. If someone gives them a negative response, the filthy rich simply refuse to acknowledge it, abstain from hearing it, and move ahead with their plan.

And if you want to be successful, you too will have to learn to never take *No* for an answer. Push, pull, harass and badger your potential customer or client until you wear down their resistance, and they finally see the light of your brilliance. And in some cases, they will buy what you're selling just to get you to shut up. But the reason doesn't matter; either way, you close the deal, get the sell, win the contract, and cram another pile of money in your bank account.

Strategy 12:
Let's Get Psychological

Most people desperately want to be loved, or at least liked by everyone; and this weakness poisons their daily lives and business practices. It also demonstrates a poor self-image, a plethora of potential psychological issues, and a misunderstanding of life in general.

You see, you are not here on earth for people to like you, although this is most certainly a common misconception. You are here to succeed, to make money, to prosper, to build a kingdom, and to get filthy rich. And if you spend much of your time worrying about what people think of you or your behavior, then you will not succeed.

Instead, you will find yourself frozen in place, fearful that your next move will offend someone or that your next statement will cause people to think badly of you. This mindset is destructive to all that you should hold dear. You must let go of it. Focus on your unique personhood as a powerful creature on God's green earth. Remember that you are head and shoulders above everyone else. Follow your path, seek your destiny, and don't worry about the opinions of others. Do what works for you, get your money, and laugh all the way to the bank.

Strategy 13:
People Are Stupid

We as a society like to think that we are continually evolving upward, and becoming more intelligent as a species. We look around at all of our technological accomplishments and tell ourselves how brilliant we must be! But the truth is that, while the top one percent of humanity's most brilliant minds can create technological wonders, the masses grow more ignorant with every passing day.

Remember the old saying commonly attributed to the great showman, P.T. Barnum: *There's a sucker born every minute.* He was quite correct. Stupid people are everywhere and all around us. If you have an unusual or questionable product, sales pitch, or service to offer to the world, you may wonder if anyone will actually buy it. But rest assured that if you present your product with gaudy wrapping paper, flashing lights, hip music, and a carefully crafted, emotionally-appealing back-story, the masses will buy what you're selling, even if it's a piece of junk. Polish a turd, splash it with perfume, push it hard, and the multitudes will eat it up.

Never overestimate the intelligence of people; most are incredibly stupid and can be easily scammed or duped. You just have to be smarter, slicker, and more cunning than they are. And, chances are, you probably are. Besides, someone is going to take advantage of them; why shouldn't it be you?

Strategy 14:
The Cunning Chameleon

A creature such as a chameleon has tremendous power to get what it wants by being all things to all people. It adapts to any and every situation with great cunning, and is therefore able to win the favor of those with whom it does business. It possesses the ability to fully apply the old principle: *When in Rome, do as the Romans*.

Wherever it finds itself, such a changeling knows how to say exactly what its listeners want to hear. It knows just how to get its enemies to let down their guard. And it has the ability to move about with great stealth, and pounce upon its victims with no warning.

By utilizing the power of a chameleon, you can pretend to be things and do things to win the favor of those with whom you are dealing. In so doing, you can more easily manipulate and take advantage of them; all of which will enhance your ability to become filthy rich.

Strategy 15:
Think on Your Feet

On the path to monetary gain and success, there are many distractions, pitfalls, and troubles. The road to riches is rarely easy, my friend. And for those of us who are focused on the ultimate goal to get filthy rich, we can sometimes become lost in the financial wilderness, distracted by the pains and challenges of life. When that happens, we may unfortunately miss out on numerous economic opportunities, and allow our competitors to seize the day. We must not permit this to happen.

I suggest you begin training yourself today to think on your feet, to be prepared for any eventuality you may face. Harden your financial muscles, fortify your defenses, and steel yourself against distractions by undertaking a rigorous regimen of exercises aimed at improving your concentration under difficult conditions.

How many times have you been in a confrontational or other high-pressure situation, and could not find the right words to say or actions to take? And then later, when the moment has passed, you suddenly realize what you should have said or could have done. How frustrating this is! Sadly, this happens to all of us throughout our lives, but there are some practical exercises to help you learn to act and speak powerfully in the moment.

For one such exercise, you will need a trusted friend to assist you. The two of you will stand facing each other, approximately three feet apart. Instruct your friend that he is to slap you firmly in the face with no prior warning, and at random times, at least three seconds but no more than fifteen seconds apart. You will begin counting backwards slowly but steadily from one hundred. As you count, your friend will then initiate the face-slapping. Your challenge will be to maintain your composure and continue to count steadily and accurately even though you are being slapped in the face at random times.

A second exercise involves the use of cold water or ice, and can be performed alone. Get in the shower and turn the water on cold. As the frigid water flows over your naked body, see how many of the fifty states you can name. Alternatively, rather than take a shower, simply grip a large ice cube in each hand, and see if you can name the fifty states *and* their capitals. As your ability to concentrate improves, you may wish to up the level of difficulty by holding the ice cubes under your armpits or in your underwear, for example.

The key is for you to learn to remain intensely focused on your goals no matter what life or your enemies throw at you. With this sort of self-discipline, you will always know exactly how to speak, act, and capitalize on the opportunities before you, regardless of the circumstances.

Strategy 16:
Volunteerism is Highly Overrated

These days everyone is talking about being a volunteer, helping the needy, and giving of time and resources to make the world a better place. This sort of pie-in-the-sky attitude sounds lovely, but it definitely does not measure up where it counts the most – on your bottom line.

Many people do volunteer work so that they get a warm and fuzzy feeling deep inside, but I warn you not to trade the beauty of cold, hard cash for some vague case of the "warm and fuzzies" which could just as well be a touch of heartburn or intestinal gas.

Bear in mind that every bit of energy, time, and money you expend helping others simply takes away from your ability to become filthy rich. Time spent feeding the hungry at a soup kitchen or mentoring inner city kids is time that could have been better used making a sale, winning a contract, closing a deal, or developing a fabulous new product. I know it can be quite difficult when it seems like everybody's doing it, but you must not give in to the peer pressure. There are already more than enough "do-gooders" in the world; we certainly don't need another one.

Stand up for your own financial freedom and the economic kingdom you are building. Volunteerism is highly overrated and can cut deeply into your profit margin, if you're not careful. You must be vigilant against it!

Strategy 17:
Shock and Awe

You probably recall the American battle plan dubbed *Shock and Awe* used by the United States in its attack upon Iraq in 2003. This clever and highly effective technique calls for an attacker to impose overwhelming dominance upon his adversary. By striking hard and fast with devastating and irresistible firepower, the enemy is quickly demoralized and defeated.

Fearlessness is an important component of this strategy. As the attacker, you must fear nothing, even when it's a situation where you really should be afraid. You must be daring and bold, willing to go out on a limb or wade into the fray with no hesitation. By employing this tactic, you will get things done, impress your peers, and devastate your competitors.

With *Shock and Awe*, you must not show weakness. You must go into every business meeting, sales pitch, conference, seminar, or competitive situation with guns blaring. If you do so, your enemies will be overwhelmed and people will be automatically drawn to your power and charisma like moths to a flame. They will want to be in your presence, work for you, or be your devoted, lifelong customers because people admire and respect any individual who displays this type of gumption.

I guarantee this strategy works; so use it today! Go on the offensive and you will destroy your competition and get filthy rich beyond your wildest dreams

Strategy 18:
Winners and Losers

In recent generations, there has been a growing trend toward down-playing the importance of winning, and the winning-at-all-costs mentality has been given a very bad name. In most of our school classrooms and organized sports, our children are taught to be mediocre. We teach them that winning is really not terribly important, and that the main thing is just to have fun. We pay lip service to the idea of striving for excellence, but our actions and attitudes say otherwise. What are our children to believe?

Let's take a quick look at reality. In every sport, competition, and business enterprise, there are a handful of winners and a surplus of losers. Take professional football, for example. When one team wins the Super Bowl, there is a tremendous amount of celebration, joy, financial reward, and fame for everyone associated with the winning team. The world glorifies the winner, stands in awe of their accomplishments, and gives them a variety of awards for their victory. They get to meet the President of the United States, ticker-tape parades are thrown in their honor, and they receive big, fat checks.

Meanwhile, all the other teams in the league are simply losers. They skulk away into the shadows as second-rate, has-beens to be forgotten until next season, when they will once again strive to be a winner. But until then, they remain failures.

Some people in this world succeed in their chosen field, and they are admired, highly respected, and make a ton of money. Meanwhile, some lead lives of mediocrity, struggling from one paycheck to the next, and others are forced to sleep on the street and rummage in garbage cans to find food.

Now, ask yourself, which would you like to be – a winner or a loser? Do you want to be just another average performer in the game of life? Or do you want to achieve greatness, conquer the world, and get filthy rich? You know the answer to the question. And to accomplish it, you must stop settling for mediocrity, and begin to strive for greatness. As coach Vince Lombardi once said, *Winning isn't everything, it's the only thing!*

We must remind ourselves and teach our children that the world consists of winners and losers, and that winning is the ultimate and only tolerable outcome. And we must also remember that losing is very bad, an utter humiliation, and completely unacceptable.

Strategy 19:
Machine vs. Man

These days, everybody seems to want to be touchy-feely and lovey-dovey. People wear their feelings out on their sleeves and pour out their hearts to anyone who will listen. Everybody thinks they can save the whales, protect the spotted owls, or safeguard the red-breasted sap-sucker. That sort of childish idealism is all well and good if you're at tea party or baking sugar cookies with your girlfriends. But it will get you absolutely nowhere in the real world.

Emotions and sentimentality are your dreaded enemies on the path to financial success. Your feelings will only distract you and get in your way. You must become emotionless like a machine, a merciless robot with no pity or compassion, and no feelings whatsoever. A computer sees only zeroes and ones; and views the entire world simply as binary code to be processed. Such a mechanism is cold-hearted, ruthless and tireless. It never sleeps and it never stops. The end result, the correct calculation, and the bottom line are the only things that matter to a machine.

In your business plan and your quest for success and riches, you must harden your heart and follow the way of the machine. This is your best chance to conquer your enemies and competitors. Metal will tear through flesh every time, and machine will conquer man in every confrontation. Be the machine.

Strategy 20:
Sacrifice Sucks but it Succeeds

You must be willing to sacrifice anything in order to become filthy rich. And I do mean *anything*. That includes quality time with your children, romance with your significant other, fun with friends, and hobbies that you enjoy. I understand that this sort of extreme sacrifice is not at all easy. And sometimes you will become weepy and sentimental, and you'll be tempted to leave work early or skip an important meeting just so that you can attend a child's ballgame or dance recital. But you must be strong and learn to walk in wisdom and objectivity. With each potential distraction that presents itself, ask yourself this vital question: *Is this going to help me become filthy rich?*

If the answer to that question is *No*, then you must walk away from the temptation, regardless of how powerful it may be. Keep your eyes focused on your long-term goal, no matter the temporary personal cost. You've given yourself a high calling – the quest for great riches – and you must stay the course, fight the good fight, and be true to yourself. Those who can do this are the ones who will become filthy rich.

Strategy 21:
Live Rich, Die Young

We live in an age when people are encouraged and pushed into longer and longer lives by the government, medical establishment, and the big drug manufacturers. They want to pump you full of pharmaceutical products, and hook you up to a slew of machines and other mechanical devices. But who benefits from all this? NOT YOU. Longer life for you only means more money for them.

Under the current system, your "golden years" are actually the part of your life when your "gold" (your financial resources) is drained from you by the woes and misfortunes of old age, poor health, and the resulting medical expenses. Politicians, drug-makers, and the medical community will laugh all the way to the bank while you trudge around on a tortuous and unending circuit of doctor appointments, blood draws, physical therapies, x-rays & scans, colonoscopies, dialysis, hip replacements and a multitude of other surgeries.

Then, eventually, you'll be shipped away to a dark and dreary nursing home where no one will visit you for months at a time. There, clad only in a pathetic gown that opens up the back, you will shuffle up and down lonely corridors in your stocking feet, with your un-wiped rear end hanging out, roaming hallways that stink of urine and week-old meatloaf.

However, those who get rich and succeed in life do NOT follow this pathway. And you must do as they do. You must train yourself to live hard and fast, and to grab hold of life TODAY with every ounce of strength you possess. Push yourself to your limits in this manner, and you will make piles of money, live on Easy Street, and fall over dead of exhaustion at a suitably early age. There will be no ten-year stint in a nursing home for you. There will be no tears and arguments among your relatives about whether or not to unhook you from a breathing machine. And there will be no medical bills piled up in excess of half a million dollars to suck every last penny out of your estate.

Heed this timely advice: Live hard and fast…and die young. You and everyone else, especially your heirs, will be happier all the way around.

Strategy 22:
Ugly Poor People

We've all heard the expression: *Money can't buy happiness*. Sadly, this saying is just something that poor people tell themselves in an effort to assuage their sorrow and poverty. It's closely related to the old wives' tale *Beauty is only skin deep*, which is an equally ridiculous axiom that ugly people rely upon. And while many people might wish these two expressions were true, alas, they are both bold-faced lies.

Deep down in their hearts, all human beings recognize and understand the accuracy and validity of the equation: Money = Happiness. It's just as true as $2 + 2 = 4$! And while some may argue vehemently against this mathematical truth, they have no solid ground upon which to stand. Anyone who answers truthfully must admit that, if given the choice, they would rather be filthy rich than poor. And to claim otherwise is an utter falsehood.

Yet, some people continue to dispute the equation by countering with the old saying: *If you don't have your health, you don't have anything*. To those people I say, yes, I agree that your health is important. But answer me this: would you rather be sick and poor, or sick and rich? Would you rather be ugly and poor, or ugly and rich? Stupid and poor, or stupid and rich? The answer, you see, is quite obvious. Case closed.

Strategy 23:
Copy Successful People

There are certain clear and obvious business patterns you can observe around the world, and especially in the United States. For example, when one network develops a breakthrough television program – such as a reality show or a cop drama – every other network quickly jumps on the bandwagon. Soon it seems as if there's one or more of these programs on every channel.

When a rock musician has a successful hit song, a country artist often quickly covers the same song, hoping to ride that gravy train. When one record label has success with a blonde-haired, chick singer, its competitors follow suit as quickly as possible. When one fast food chain hits upon a new and popular offering, all the others immediately develop their own, similar product. This is repeated over and over, and it's a concept that makes plenty of sense.

You want to get filthy rich? It's not necessary to reinvent the wheel. Simply look around at products and services that are already highly successful, and then copy them. Take someone else's money-making idea, put your own little twist to it, and soon you too will be sharing in the wealth.

Strategy 24:
Greed is Good

For decades, we have been brainwashed by our culture into believing that there is something inherently wrong about being greedy. Greed has been given a bad name, and as a result, much of our drive to succeed and conquer has been suppressed, and in some cases eliminated. As this philosophy spreads, we become weaker as individuals and as a nation.

The opposite of greed is generosity, the enemy of financial success. You must realize that every time you freely give away your time, money or possessions, your financial kingdom takes a big step backwards. I am not saying there is never time to give; sometimes giving can be very beneficial to your own goals, especially when it persuades people to support your efforts to get rich. I suggest you give only when it is to your advantage.

What is truly wrong with wanting and having more? Nothing. Is it bad to stockpile great heaps of money and possessions? Absolutely not. Who doesn't want to have loads of cool stuff that make them the envy of their friends and neighbors? Everyone does, of course, but many people are afraid to admit it because they've been incorrectly informed all of their lives.

This is such a terrible shame because greed is a powerhouse motivator that can make things happen for you. It can often be the most effective, driving force to push you beyond your limits and into greatness. So don't listen to the naysayers. Don't deny the sheer glory of greed. Use it to your advantage!

41

Strategy 25:
Not Enough to Go Around

When it comes to wealth and success, some foolish people say that there is more than enough to go around for everyone. They urge you to share the wealth and warn you not to be greedy. But they're dead wrong. There will always be the "haves" and the "have-nots" because that's the way the world is set up. There has never been and never will be a time when everyone is rich and has plenty of what they need or want. Even Jesus alluded to this fact when He said that we would always have the poor with us.

Don't fall into the trap of popular opinion or socialistic or communistic values. According to the laws of physics, economics, and reality, it is impossible for everyone to be filthy rich or have more than enough of the most valuable things like money, opportunity, and resources.

Therefore, if you're wise, you'd best get yours now. Grab hold of every material possession you can, and hoard any excess you're able to accumulate. Then, when the time is right, you'll be able to add to your monetary fortune by selling that surplus to those in need when the demand is at its peak. The intelligent and aggressive business-person will understand that there is not enough to go around, and will act accordingly.

Strategy 26:
Being Poor is Worse than Death

At least when you're dead, you're at peace. But when you live in the poorhouse, there is no peace. Every day is a heart-breaking struggle to scrape together a few more pennies to make your rent, pay your electric bill, put food on the table, and clothe your children. Living in abject poverty means you go to bed every night with a gnawing in your gut, not only from physical hunger, but from the knowledge that tomorrow will likely be no better than today.

While the rich dine on roast duck and $40-per-pound Gorau Glas bleu cheese; the poor share a bag of pork rinds, gnaw on a block of government cheese, and curse the day they were born. Such is the horrible disparity in America; and, trust me; you most definitely want to be on the winning side of that deadly, dividing line. It is definitely no fun when the iron door of poverty slams shut on you.

Therefore, you must find a way to rise up out of the financial hole in which you find yourself. And you *can* do it! Think, study and research. Work harder than ever before. And most importantly, implement the brilliant and highly effective strategies described in this book. Then, and only then, will you be on your way to supremacy over the poor, huddled masses, and firmly ensconced in the ranks of the filthy rich!

Strategy 27:
Learn from History

Consider the richest people in the world. How do you think almost every single one of them got that way? I guarantee the answer is one of two possibilities: (1) they were born into wealth with a silver spoon in their mouth; or (2) they became filthy rich by applying the strategies listed in this book. There are very few other avenues to riches. If you think you're going to win the lottery or somehow just fall into great wealth through a fluke, then you are a complete fool.

Take a long look at the families who live in luxury and vast wealth in the world today. Their lives have been transformed thanks to their money-grubbing, filthy rich ancestors. And now their children are the ones who will be born with a silver spoon, to be followed by their children, their children's children, and so forth and so on. You see, once you accumulate great wealth and power, you and your descendants will likely retain those riches and reap the benefits for a very long time. And, typically, the only way you will ever lose your wealth is by being extremely stupid or completely irresponsible with your money and investments.

Now consider these questions: Wouldn't you like to give your family the greatest gift of all by setting them up with riches, prestige, and power for generations? Of course you would. And this is precisely what all the wealthy people in the world have done throughout the ages. Learn from their example, learn from history, and follow their lead. You will be glad you did.

Strategy 28:
The New Golden Rule

The ancient Golden Rule – *Do unto others as you would have them do unto you* – is noble and altruistic, but it will in no way aid your quest for riches. In fact, the concept runs totally contrary to your all-important plan to accumulate greater wealth for yourself while denying monetary gain to others.

I maintain it's time for a New Golden Rule, one properly suited for the mindset and lifestyle of the filthy rich: *Do unto others such that you can take what is theirs.* That is, do whatever is necessary to obtain the things that other people possess. This can be accomplished through a wide variety of techniques and strategies such as those I have described in this book.

First, you must study your target to discover what method will be most effective for their personality type. For some, you may only need to sweet-talk them gently, win them over with fake kindness, and these soft-hearted fools will easily allow you to take advantage of them.

Others may imagine themselves too clever to be taken in by your mushy stories and kind words. For these customers, clients, or competitors, you must be even cleverer than they are. You must deceive with great cunning by developing intricate business plans to capitalize on their weaknesses, manipulating fine print to trap them, or creating complex agreements they cannot possibly decipher.

In addition, there are other people who can only be conquered via sheer force and power. They must be out-muscled by whatever means necessary. Some can be verbally berated or humiliated into compliance, while others may require a full frontal business attack, perhaps via some sort of scam, under-handed setup, or by way of hostile takeover.

Some of your victims may present a strong front at first, but you will discover that many of them actually fear conflict of any type and will avoid confrontation by all means. By implementing a business strategy such as *Shock and Awe*, for example, you will quickly have these weaklings eating out of your hand. By being stronger and more forceful than they are, you will soon be in command of all that was once theirs: raw materials, capital goods, customers, sphere of influence, and their very livelihood.

And always remember this: For every competitor you drive out of business – by whatever methodology you utilize – you are one rung higher on the ladder of success, and that much closer to being filthy rich.

Strategy 29:
The Land of Unicorns

I'm sorry, Dorothy, but this isn't Kansas. And we do not live in a sweet and wonderful world of kitty cats, rainbows, sparkles and unicorns. Furthermore, everybody isn't nice, timid, and generous; and things don't magically work out fine in the end. Not even close. This world is a dangerous, dog-eat-dog nightmare kennel where the mediocre get trampled on and the weak get euthanized.

I implore you not to walk around with stars in your eyes, thinking that you can succeed as a nice guy. Nice guys may come in first in The Land of Unicorns, but here in the real world, things follow the more tried, true and reliable principle: *Nice guys finish last.* If they finish at all, that is.

So, don't ever allow yourself to be a nice guy; instead, be vicious. Don't be accommodating; be demanding. Don't be starry-eyed like a child; be steely-eyed like an angry gladiator. And the only unicorn you should ever believe in is the one upon which you'll be mounted in all your filthy rich glory; the one with the razor-sharp horn that you will use to pierce through the hearts and flesh of your competitors, and gut those who stand in your way on the path to great riches and success.

Strategy 30:
Money Meditation

Studies have proven repeatedly that meditation is good for the mind and body. Therefore, I urge you to take a few moments to reflect on what's really important in your life. I close this book with my own personal mantra, a few simple, yet profound words of wisdom.

Each day, early in the morning, just before the stock market opens, let the beauty of all of God's creation fill your soul. Muse and meditate on the verses below. Repeat them out loud to yourself, over and over and over again, until you've memorized them, and they permeate the deepest regions of your very being…

My children are precious,
As long as they do not require my attention;
My spouse is adorable,
As long as she abides by the prenuptial agreement;
The world is such a beautiful place,
As long as it does not distract me from my work;
I am at peace with the Universe,
As long as my money is safe;
My conscience is clear and clean,
As long as I am filthy rich.

www.ingramcontent.com/pod-product-compliance
Lightning Source LLC
Chambersburg PA
CBHW071744020426
42331CB00008B/2175